T0071109

Singing by Numbers

Bob Chilcott

for SATB and piano

MUSIC DEPARTMENT

OXFORD
UNIVERSITY PRESS

Singing by Numbers is a collection of seven songs about singing, commissioned by the Midland Branch of the Association of British Choral Directors, in celebration of the 10th birthday convention of the ABCD, held in Birmingham, August 1995.

I designed this suite to be fun, easy to perform, and to include as many different vocal scorings as possible within its relatively short duration. The word 'number' in the title can either refer to a number of people singing together, or to the word 'number' meaning a song, or to the fact that the songs can be performed separately, as a whole, and in any order—in other words, in any number of ways!

Complete duration: *c.*10 minutes

Bob Chilcott
July 1995

SINGING BY NUMBERS

No. 1 Sing we now merrily

Thomas Ravenscroft (?*c*.1582–*c*.1635)

BOB CHILCOTT

Commissioned by the Association of British Choral Directors Midland Region for the ABCD 10th Anniversary Convention, and first performed at the Convention on 27th August 1995.

This piece is scored for 2 flutes, 2 oboes, 2 clarinets, 2 bassoons, 2 horns, 2 trumpets and strings; scores and instrumental parts are available from the publisher's Hire Library.

Printed in Great Britain

OXFORD UNIVERSITY PRESS, MUSIC DEPARTMENT, GREAT CLARENDON STREET, OXFORD OX2 6DP

9
Hey - ho! Hey - ho! Hey - ho! Hey - ho!
sffz f
8va
sffz
8va
13
Hey - ho! Let them take care that list to spare, for
stacc. and driving
17
I will not do so. Who can sing so mer - ry a

note as he that can - not change a groat?
Hey - ho!
Hey - ho!
Hey-ho!
Hey - ho!
Hey - ho!
Attacca No. 2
Hey - ho!

No. 2 The singing of birds

From *The Song of Solomon*

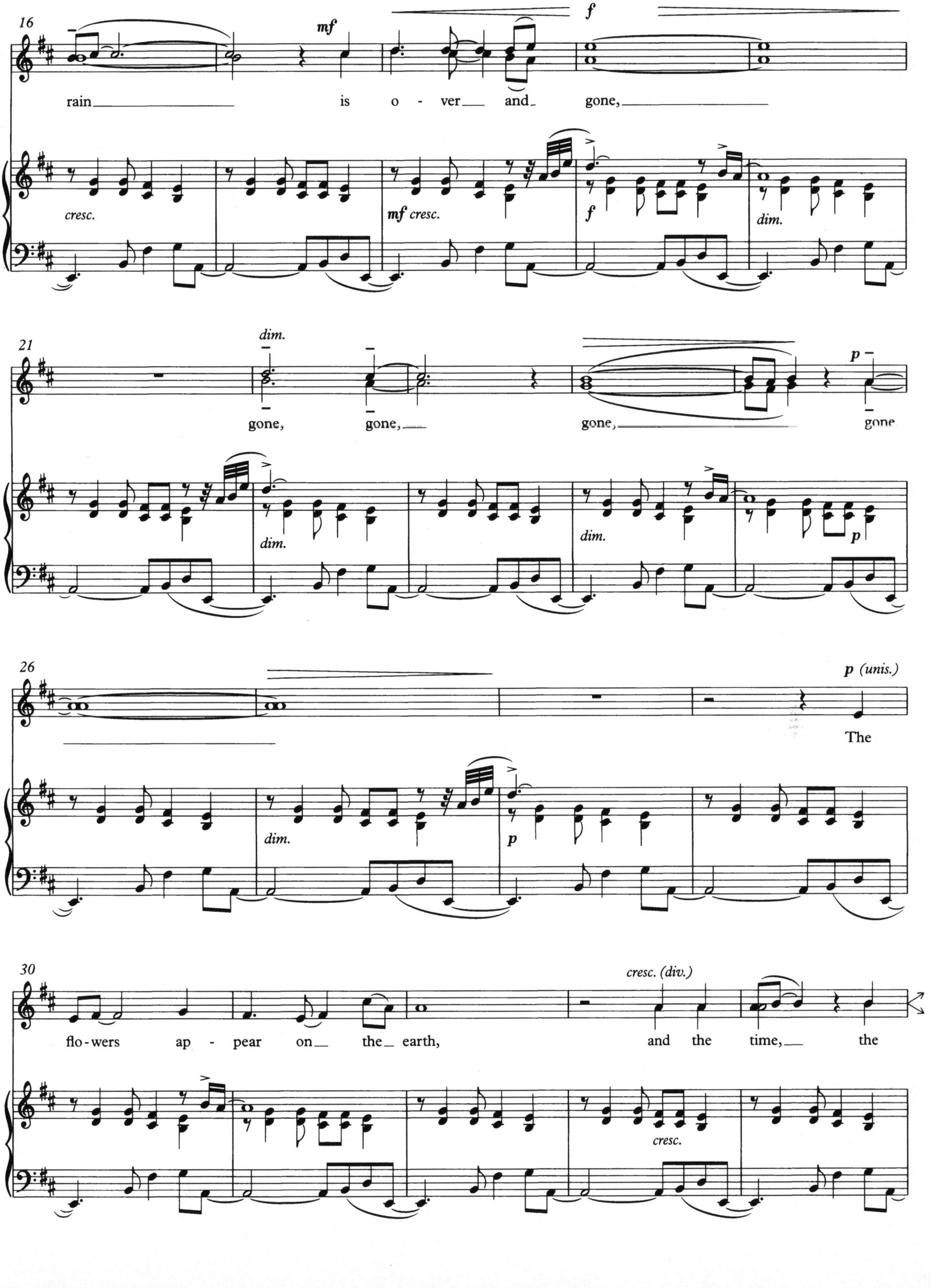
16
mf
f
rain is o - ver and gone,
cresc.
mf cresc.
f
dim.
21
dim.
p
gone, gone, gone, gone
dim.
dim.
p
26
p (unis.)
The
dim.
p
30
cresc. (div.)
flo-wers ap - pear on the earth, and the time, the
cresc.

S.1
S.2
time of the sing - ing of birds, the sing - ing of
time, the sing - ing of birds, the
cresc.
f
birds, the sing - ing of birds
sing - ing of birds, of birds
dim.
is come, come, come, come.
p
rit.
slower
Attacca No. 3
dim. e rit.
pp

No. 3 Hey down a down!

Thomas Ravenscroft (?c.1582–c.1635)

17
2.
af - ter me,
With hey down a down,
sffz
ff
24
ff
Troll, troll the ber - ry, Drink and be mer - ry, Troll, troll the ber - ry,
ff
30
Drink and be mer - ry.
ff
sffz

No. 4 Cruet MacNightshade

Spike Milligan (b. 1918)

*Should be sung with a short *portamento* up to the first note.

Text from *A Book of Goblins* by Spike Milligan.

11
dee dee dee dee dee dee dee dee dee dee dee dee dee
la la la dee dee dee dee dee dee dee dee dee dee dee dee dee
mf espress.
I al-ways look up when sing - ing out in the
la la la la la la la la la
mf espress.
16
mf espress.
La de da de da
mp
la la la la la la la la la la la la la la la la la la
f mf
street you see. La de da de da
mp
la la la la la la la la la la
mf espress.
mp
f mf

22
La de da dee dee
la la la la la la la la la la la la la
mf espress.
La de da dee dee Be -
la la la la la la la la
mf espress.
27
dee dee dee dee dee dee dee dee dee dee dee dee dee
dee dee dee dee dee dee dee dee dee dee dee dee dee
- cause of late they have been throw-ing buck-ets of wa - ter o - ver
la la la la la la la

32
mp
la la la la la
la la la la la la la la la la
me.
f mf
La de da de da
la la la la la la
la la la la la la la la la la
la la la la la la la la la la

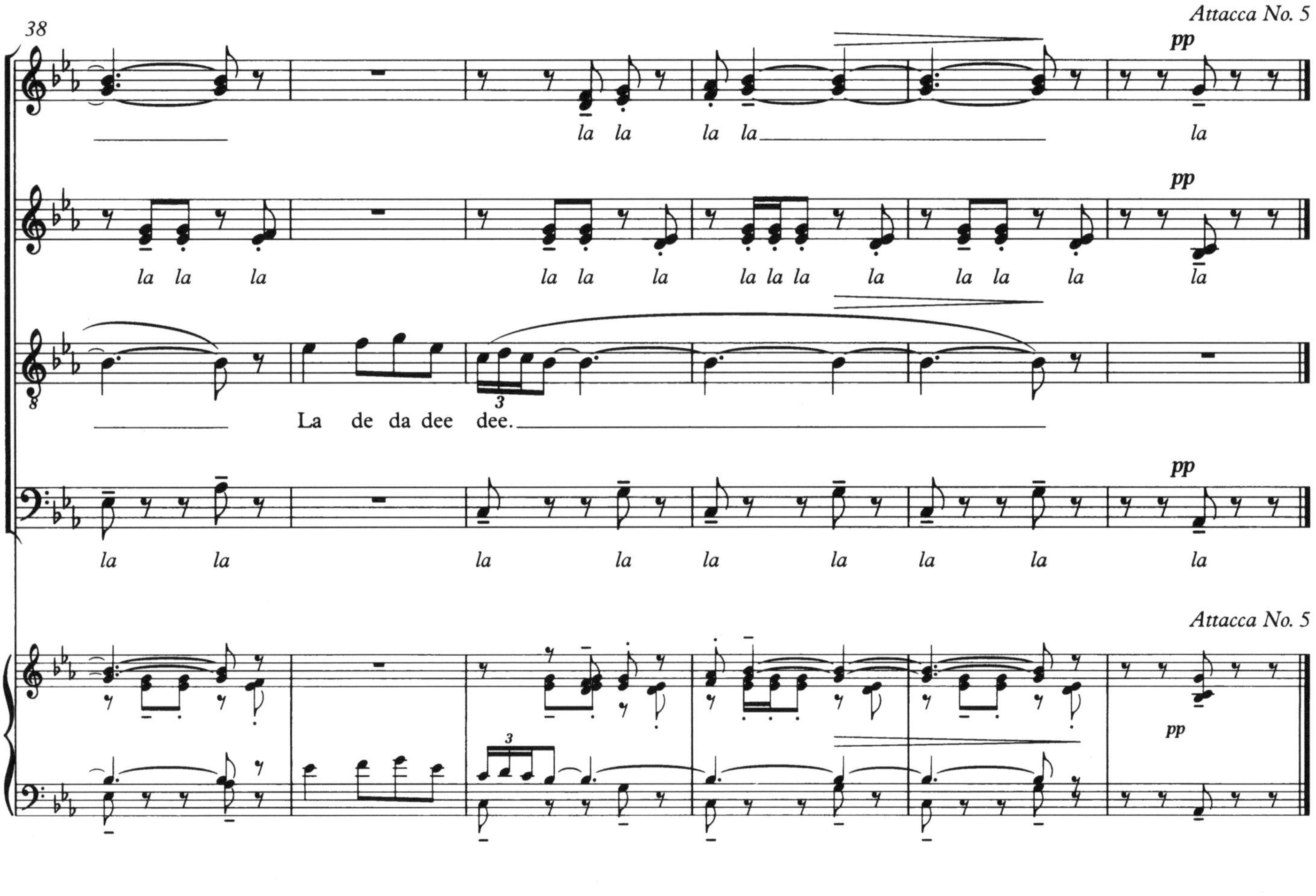
38
Attacca No. 5
pp
la la la la la
la la la la la la la la la la la la la
La de da dee dee.
la la la la la la la la la
Attacca No. 5
pp

No. 5 Sing you now

Thomas Ravenscroft (?*c.*1582–*c.*1635)

21
poco rit.
ppp
sing ye; And as I sing, sing ye;
ppp
And as I sing, sing ye;
poco rit.
ppp
28
a tempo
p poco più espress.
poco rit.
a tempo
So shall we well a-gree, two parts in u-ni-ty.
p poco più espress.
So shall we well a-gree, two parts in u-ni-ty.
a tempo
poco rit.
a tempo
p poco più espress.
pp
35
(TUTTI)
pp
a bit slower
ppp
sing you now sing you now sing you now.
a bit slower
ppp

No. 6 Everyone sang

Siegfried Sassoon (1886–1967)

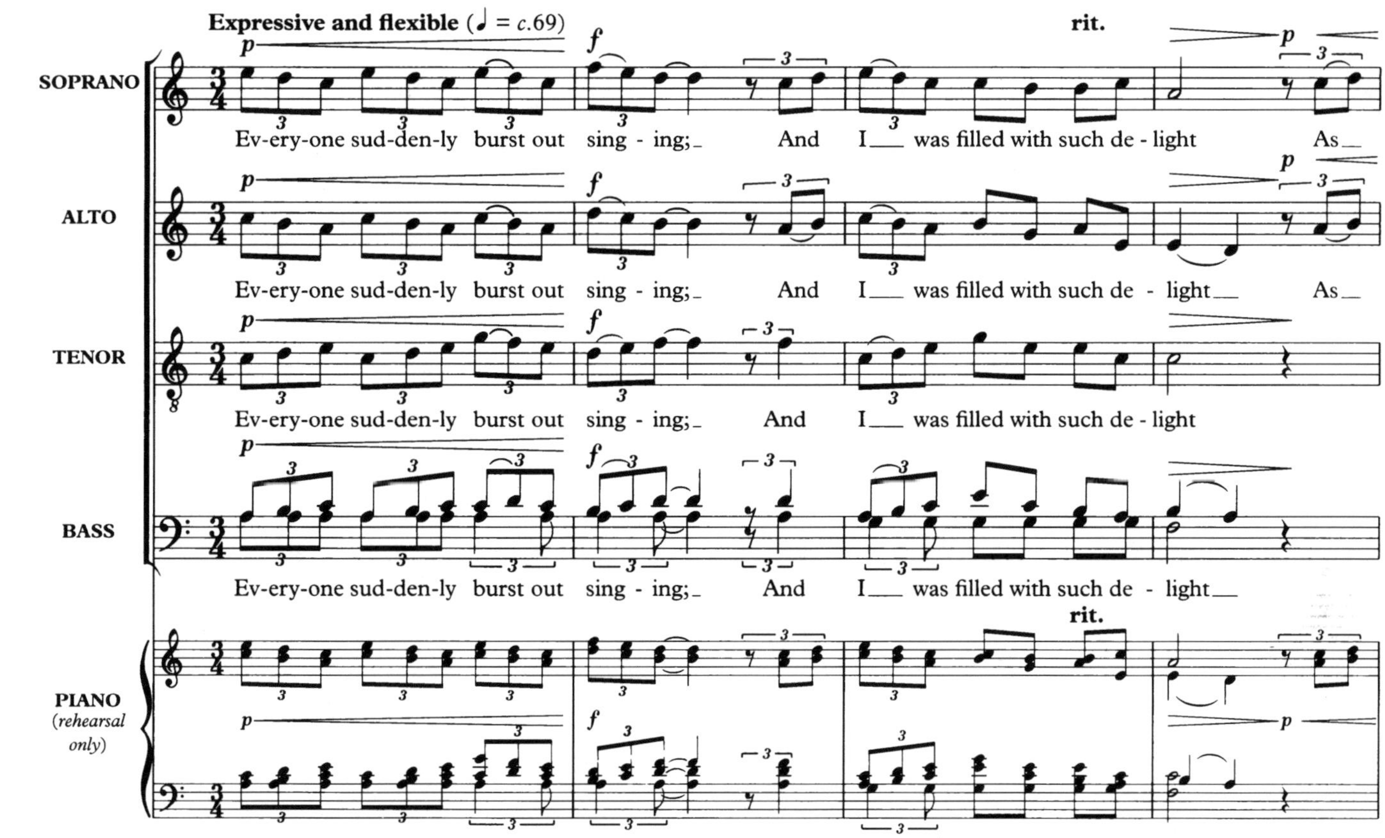

Text used by kind permission of George Sassoon.

poco rit.
slower
rit.
pick up tempo
dark-green fields; on, on, and out of sight. Ev-ery-one's voice was sud-den-ly
dark-green fields; on, on, out of sight. Ev-ery-one's voice was sud-den-ly
dark-green fields; on, on, out of sight. Ev-ery-one's voice was sud-den-ly
dark-green fields; on, on, out of sight. Ev-ery-one's voice was sud-den-ly
poco rit.
slower
rit.
pick up tempo
mf dolce
mp espress.
lift - ed; And beau - ty came like the set-ting sun: My heart was sha-ken with tears; and hor-ror
lift - ed; And beau - ty came like the set-ting sun: My heart was sha-ken with tears; and hor-ror
lift - ed; And beau - ty came like the set-ting sun: My heart was sha-ken with tears; and hor-ror
lift - ed; And beau - ty came like the set-ting sun: My heart was sha-ken with tears; and hor-ror
mf dolce
mp espress.

19
rit. e dim.
slower
rit.
p
mp espress.
dolce
drift-ed a-way, drift-ed a-way, drift-ed a-way, a - way . . . O,__ but Ev - ery - one__ was a
drift-ed, drift-ed a-way, drift-ed a - way, drif-ted a - way . . . O,__ but Ev - ery - one__ was a
drift - ed__ a - way, a - way . . . O,__ but Ev - ery - one__ was a
drift - ed,__ drift - ed,__
drift - ed__ a - way . . . O,__ but Ev - ery - one__ was a
23
slow
Attacca No. 7
mp dolce
pp
bird; and the song__ was word-less;__ the sing-ing__ will ne - ver__ be done.
bird; and the song__ was word-less;__ the sing-ing__ will ne - ver__ be done.
bird; the song__ was word-less;__ the sing-ing__ will ne - ver__ be done.
bird; the song__ was word-less;__ the sing-ing__ will ne - ver__ be done.

No. 7 Hey down a down / Sing with thy mouth

Thomas Ravenscroft (?*c*.1582–*c*.1635)

14
1.
2.
af - ter me,
af - ter me,
With hey down a down,
ff
sffz
ff
24
ff
Troll, troll the ber - ry, Drink and be mer - ry, Troll, troll the ber - ry, Drink
ff
ff
31
and be mer-ry.
f
Sing with thy mouth,
f
ff
sffz
8va

37
Sing with thy heart, Like faith - ful friends sing 'Loth to de -
sffz
8va
42
- part.' Sing, sing, sing, sing, sing, sing,
sffz
f
8va
sffz
8va
47
sing, sing, Though friends to - ge ther may not al - ways re -
f
f
stacc. and driving
f

Printed and bound in Great Britain by
Caligraving Limited Thetford Norfolk